MOMENTS
AND
MEMORIES

Wykid Concepts

In Memory of:

LCPL Rylee J McCollum USMC

02.26.2001 KIA 08.26.2021

Til Valhalla

Thank you for taking the time to read my writings!

My name is Jim McCollum. A cowboy-carpenter-poet!
I am a lifelong Wyoming kid, hence the name Wykid Concepts.
I am Wyoming through and through!

I hope you enjoy sharing my journey.

TABLE OF CONTENTS

#remembertheirnames

Honor the 13 Fallen

LCPL RYLEE J McCOLLUM

LCPL KAREEM M NIKOUI

LCPL DAVID L ESPINOZA

LCPL DYLAN R MEROLA

LCPL JARED M SCHMITZ

CPL HUNTER LOPEZ

CPL DAEGAN W PAGE

CPL HUMBERTO A SANCHEZ

SGT JOHANNY ROSARIO PICHARDO

SGT NICOLE GEE

SSGT DARIN T HOOVER

NAVY CORPSMAN MAX SOVIAK

ARMY SSGT RYAN C KNAUSS

PLEASE CLOSE THE GATE

Welcome to Wyoming
I hope you enjoy your stay
You'll find life is a little simpler here
We'd really like to keep things that way
Nestled in the Rocky Mountains
Jagged peaks and rolling plains
Unforgettable landmarks
Our Western history remains
Cattle dot the landscape
Cowboys still ride the range
Although we're changing with the times
Much remains the same
For those of us who call Her home
We wear the colors proud
It isn't hard to find a Poke fan
Standing in a crowd
Brown and Gold and Steamboat
Frontier Days and Chris Ledoux
From the Tetons down to Vedauwoo
We're Wyoming through and through
Living high in God's Country
Didn't happen by mistake
I hope you enjoyed your visit
When you leave, please close the gate.
Wykid

WATCHING HER

I watch her slowly dying
She couldn't stand the test of time
Progress takes its toll on her
In both concept and design
Her physical appearance
Giving way to modern flare
Faces once familiar
They are no longer there
The values that made her feel like home
Long ago taking a left hand turn
With no regard to lasting effects
Of lessons to be learned
I remember her from yesterdays
Simplicity by design
Her innocence and beauty
Still captivate my mind
She taught me about love and life
Her people made me whole
Liberalism and politics
Are killing Jackson Hole.
Wykid

RISE FROM THE ASHES

(Hoback Ranches 2018)
Was it a strike of a match or the flick of a Bic
A well-fed fire or a few random sticks?
Did you think of the dangers
While warming your hands?
The enveloping tinder box or adjacent dry lands
Was an effort exerted to snuff out your fire
Or did half-hearted ignorance lead to my ire?
I question your character
I question your heart
Does your conscience rest easy in the wake of this start
Landscapes no longer
Forever transformed
Lives permanently altered with the loss of our homes
You can't know the heartache your actions imposed
On those in the ranches
Our lives predisposed
My heart is heavy for my neighbors and friends
I hurt for my father as he's nearing the end
You cannot fathom the pain you have caused
You'll never know this incredible loss.
Wykid

REBUILD

The sun sits a little higher in the southern sky
Its warmth is recognized and welcomed
Dropping the tailgate, I sit in silence
Thinking of winter's impending end
So much to do, so little time
I add stress where it doesn't belong
I'll make it happen
I welcome the challenge
It's just been a little prolonged
With each passing day, my spirit is lifted
Cold, snowy days will be a thing of the past
New growth of Aspens, grasses and sage
Greener landscapes, open and vast
I look forward to evenings shared on the deck
Sharing time and drinks with some of you
Steaks and burgers sizzling out on the grill
Worries become seldom and few
Seeing dad on the porch swing enjoying the day
His camera close by his side
Sharing the dream that he shared with me
Along with love, compassion and pride.
Wykid

MONTANA MUSING

Somewhere along the Gallatin River
Steep canyon walls with rock outcroppings and trees
I took a deep breath
Let it out slowly
I had a conversation with me
About the things that truly matter
Beyond what my mind lets me see
The people
The places
The times and the moments
The experiences that in time come to be
What it is that I want,
What it is that I get
Are often separated by the extremes
A heart filled with love
Overlooked and unshared
I try hard to analyze what it means
Oh, woe is me
Doesn't hang around often
Nose to the grindstone
I forge on ahead
But still, I think of the romance
And someone lying next to me, in the same bed
I complicate my own efforts
Oversharing my thoughts and my dreams
It is what it is,
I am who I am
Full disclosure,
There is no in-between
Today, I pulled off of the highway
The miles weren't going anywhere
I jotted down a few lines,
Took a couple of pictures

For a minute,
I let myself care
I took in the sights, the sounds, and the feelings
I let go of the thoughts preconceived
I smiled,
Accepting life's blessings
And the love I've already received.
Wykid

LENSES

I wonder what my children see
When I'm viewed from behind their lens
Do they find me as I think I am?
As their father and their friend?
I'm certain views are similar
I'm sure they differ just the same
Have I made them proud of me?
Do they proudly speak my name?
To view myself through my mind's eye
I've struggled through the years
Duality as a parent, as mom and dad
Has brought about many tears
At times, I felt I was failing
Unable to give what they deserved
Going without, to give them something
Keeping my own needs reserved
I hope they see who I wanted to be
I hope they know that they make me proud
There are many things I wish I would have said
Things never spoken out loud
I imagine they see the hard-ass,
Stubborn in my own convictions
Allowing for freedoms until I pulled back the reins
Freedoms come with restrictions
They grew up hard
They grew up fast
They grew up embracing the fight
They learned compassion
They learned to give
They learned to do what is right
When the curtain falls on my story
When there are no more acts in my play
Will they smile in my memory,

The way they smile for me today?
If life has a sense of humor
They'll stick a middle finger in the air
Saying, "I love you dad, you S.O.B."
Then I'll know that they care!
Wykid

MOUNTAIN MAGIC

Peach Crown in an ice-filled glass
Night closing in on the day
Reminiscing about days gone by
Dreams that have come and gone
Those dreams that stayed
Stories and laughter filling the air
Smoke lazily drifts in the breeze
I don't ask for much
But I sure appreciate
Times and moments like these
Carefree conversations
Some coming from the heart
Beginnings and endings
Not knowing what lies ahead
Threads that keep life from coming apart
There's a magic in the mountains
Unfiltered skies revealing the stars
Finding peace in the blanket of darkness
Erasing past pain and scars.
Wykid

UNWINDING

Tell me about your morning
Did you sleep well last night?
Have you had a cup of coffee yet
To start the day off right?
I'm sure your day is busy
With a list of things to do
I just wanted to say good morning
As my thoughts were all of you
When today's hours have passed you by
And you're sitting at home tonight
Maybe you can grab a blanket,
Curling up in a chair
Sitting in the glow of candlelight
Watch the shadows dancing
Close your eyes,
What do you see?
Listen to the silence
What do you hear?
Can you share it with me?
My mind has traveled 1000 miles
As I picture you sitting there
Smiling
Relaxed
Slowly unwinding
Without a worry or a care.
Wykid

CRAVINGS

I crave the touch that lingers
The hug that doesn't let go
Her scent remaining
Long after she's gone
Her kisses, soft and slow
Fingers laced together
Her hand fits in mine like a glove
Smiles shared
Eyes engaging
A prelude to falling in love
Fingers tracing her body
Memorizing every line and curve
Pausing to gaze,
Getting lost in the moment
Content to watch and observe
My lips are wanting to taste her
Desires are burning within
Massaging her,
As she lay naked before me
Feeling the warmth of her skin
Leaning down to kiss her bare shoulder
My fingers run through her hair
She is sleeping
I hope she dreams of me
I love the time that we share.
Wykid

UNTRAVELED ROAD

I walk into the fire
Encircled by the flames
Surroundings all too familiar
The song remains the same
Questions arise
Of love and life
How did things come to be?
Did I choose the path that I'm on
Or did this path choose me?
There have been times I've slipped and stumbled
Head down on bended knee
Not knowing where I'm going
The future left unseen
I've embraced the lonely comforts
Familiarity I've felt before
The numbness slowly fading
Leaving me wanting more
I found more in conversation
I found more in the light of another's eyes
I found more,
A rediscovery
In the truths that I surmise
Where will this journey take me?
I'm not certain
I'm unsure
Each step I take on the road not traveled
Is one step closer to her.
Wykid

PROJECTIONS

I wrap myself up in the romance
I like the way it feels
Fantasies and projections
I know it isn't real
For a moment,
I can live it
The laughter, hopes and dreams
Time with her
Time together
Playing out in different scenes
Long after I put the pencil down
Closing the journal on the day
I wonder if my words reached her
Was there more that I could say?
Wykid

DIRT ROAD REFLECTIONS

Hey you, yeah you
The woman on my mind
How's the world been treating you?
I hope that it's been kind
I think about you often
I thought of giving you a call
I've memorized your number
Hell, I remember it all
As for me, I can't complain
The world blesses me each day
I must admit, I've been a little lonely
Since you went away
I took a drive down that old dirt road
The Aspen holds onto the scars
Where we carved in our initials
Where we made love under the stars
Today I took the dog for a ride
We stopped to say hi to you
Kneeling at your granite headstone
I shed a tear or two
I hope you know I miss you
I should have shown you how much I care
You were so strong and vibrant
I thought you'd always be there.
Wykid

THE SCENT OF A WOMAN

The scent of a woman, intoxicating
The touch of her lips feeds desires
The touch of her skin warms the passion
The life in her eyes fuels the fire
The scent of a woman, perfume sweet and warm
The fragrance of her flesh, soft and mild
Musky scent of sweat, sweet and subtle
Womanhood, animalistic, primal, and wild
The touch of her lips, I'm drifting away
Caught up in dreams, day and night
Her lips on mine, my skin, my flesh
The world stops and all feels right
The softness of her skin, warm and tender
On bended knee, I serve my queen
Protecting her from pain and harm
A commitment of depths unseen
The life in her eyes contagious
A wild and passionate soul
A soaring spirit of confidence
Creating her beautiful glow.
Wykid

BENEATH THE SURFACE

She shared with me her story
At times it broke my heart
To know that she'd been hurting
Her world had come apart
I learned from her, her passions
Touched the surface of her life
Never dwelling in too deeply
She'll decide when that feels right
I shared with her my journey
Of the life I left behind
She did not pass down judgment
As I spoke from heart and mind
I know she couldn't see me
When I smiled as she wrote
She couldn't feel my heartache
When I cried from words she spoke
I wish I had the answers
To all the questions in my head
I wonder if she thought of me
When night beckoned her to bed.
Wykid

SHOTGUN BLASTS
AND MOMENTS THAT LAST

A little summer fun
With a woman and her gun
Tripping pigeons and watching them disappear
A cooler full of goodies
Warm enough to shed the hoodies
Wyoming sun, it's the perfect time of year
In between the shotgun blasts
We speak of today, tomorrow, the past
Enjoying a little time away
I love this time together
The time is ours until whenever
Until then, I am happy here today
Picking up ejected shells
Thinking of the sounds and smells
Of the forest, the Aspens and the sage
Could this day get any better?
It's been perfect to the letter
Our story, I can't wait to turn the page
Walking to a little stream
We sit down where the grass is green
Lying back, we stare into the sky
I take her hand in mine
Our fingers intertwined
In total silence, neither knowing why
I turn to look her way
Just in time to hear her say
I'm having fun, but I would like a kiss
That was all it took
Another chapter in our book
These are the things I really miss
For you see, it's just a tale
But I can feel it just as well

So real, so vivid in my mind
These dreams start through conversation
But their final destination
Words on paper, stories trapped in time.
Wykid

GOOD MORNING

Quiet darkness surrounds me
A blanket holds the heat
I smile, movement beside me
My skin warming her cold feet
A giggle, so sweet to hear her
Her arm resting on my chest
A soft kiss on my right ear
Mornings with her are truly the best.
Wykid

PRISMS

Bare feet with shiny polish
In the shallows of the stream
The brilliant red, eye-catching
Through waters prismatic gleem
He studies more, the photograph
Wonders of the story within
It doesn't matter, he wasn't there
But in his mind she's there, with him.
Wykid

TIME AND TENDERNESS

A little time and tenderness
A touch once in awhile
A kiss on the cheek, an "I love you"
A reason for him to smile
A wanting to be needed
To know that he's her man
The man she can depend on
Who will listen and understand
A little time and tenderness
Holding his hand in yours
A woman he can count on
When hardships are endured
A hug, there's nothing better
It lets him know you care
To you, he knows he matters
When a loving hug is shared
A little time and tenderness
To right the wayward ship
He craves the love you give him
And the taste of your sweet lips.
Wykid

INNOCENCE

Let's go splash in puddles
Or catch snowflakes on our tongues
Look for 4-leafed clovers
Like we did when we were young
Let's spend late nights talking
Just to share each other's time
Let's pass silly love notes
One that says "Will you be mine?"
Let's hold hands in summer
Let's plant flowers in the spring
Let's go sledding in the winter
Enjoy the colors that fall brings
Let's sit across the table
Coffee cup in hand
Let me love you as a woman
Let me know that I'm your man
Let me always show you
That you have nothing to fear
Let my love surround you
I'm so thankful you are here.
Wykid

SLOW RIDE

The excitement unrelenting
As she dances around his mind
Anxious for her conversation
His happiness unconfined
Getting lost in his own visions
Getting lost in his own thoughts
Losing sight of what's important
The lessons life has taught
Listen to her intently
Hear the things she has to say
Slow time down, don't go too fast
Enjoy the time with her today
Worry and overthinking
Detrimental to points of view
Appreciate her taking time
To share herself with you
Can I abide by my own logic?
Live by the very words I say?
You've got one shot to get it right
Or risk pushing her away.
Wykid

UNSPOKEN

Sitting on the bed
She's brushing polish on her toes
She shares with him her laughter
She wrinkles up her nose
She wears boxers and black tank top
The polish Candy Apple Red
She concentrates on painting
As she listens to what is said
He keeps it light and simple
Though he has a lot to say
So much he wants to tell her
Should he wait another day?
She holds a foot before him
He grasps it gently and begins to blow
He kisses the bottom of her foot
He wonders if she knows
She has seen him at his weakest
Vulnerable, open, and scared
Together, sharing intimate thoughts
Hearts and souls were bared
The comfort felt between them
One of compassion, loyalty, and trust
Although wants and desires surround him
He abstains from temptation and lust
The hardest words he has to say
Are the ones still left unspoken
No rhyme or reason for apprehension and fear
Just the chance a heart may be broken
A few more strokes, singing "This Little Piggy"
She raises her foot to him
He blows on the polish, kissing her toes
Something he does for her now and again
Like cooking her dinner when she's had a long day

Cleaning up just to save her the time
Preparing an evening for her to relax
With bubble bath, candles, and wine
A message for no reason
A story to put her to bed
He laughs at himself, he did it again
Another day with words left unsaid
He lays his head on his pillow
He blows kisses to her in the night
He whispers, "I love you, I'll be with you soon."
Then he quietly turns out the lights.
Wykid

BEAUTY AND THE BEAST

There is no innocence
In the way he thinks of her
No apologies
No regrets
He expresses thoughts through words
The beast within awakened
It slowly begins to stir
The beast of love and passion
Knowing the beauty he's found in her
A man among men
A fighter
Wondering where that man has been
Who is this man, uncertain?
He seeks the warrior he buried within
He angers himself
Disappointed
Fighting to get his emotions in check
The battle he fights inside his head
Like a noose around his neck
Analytical and creative
It's like black is fighting white
A calmness in his thinking
Is what he's hoping for tonight
Today he looks within himself
To calm the storm at the very least
She comforts him with kindness
Beauty and the Beast.
Wykid

THE PEACEFUL CALM

There's a peaceful calm, a comfort
She still lingers in my mind
Disregarding the reality
Casting away the time
The smile—I can't ignore the smile
Captivated at the very first glance
Vivacious, exciting, and engaging
Her beauty, simply enhanced
Her eyes, so warm and inviting
There's adventure in her gaze
I imagine the heaven behind them
I could look into them for days
Framing her face are her long locks of hair
A picture-perfect view
Stylish changes in photographs
Sporting a color brand-new
She lingers uncontested
There's no image to take her place
Cooling her feet in a cool mountain stream
Sunglasses adorning her face
Feet on the dashboard, soaking up rays
Enjoying the warm summer sun
A day on the river, a day on the lake
A day in the mountains for fun
There's a peaceful calm, a comfort
I love the way she lingers
The smiles subside for a moment
I see her slip through my fingers.
Wykid

NIGHTFALL

Night has fallen peacefully
A blanket our cocoon
You're in my arms; I'm in yours
Candles lightning the room
A chance to be together
No distractions or concerns
Music playing soft and low
The fire slowly burns
Our fingers laced together
Our legs are intertwined
My hand is resting on your breast
Your head resting on mine
We talk about the evening
We share the day's events
We speak about the future
And the good times we have spent
A comfort falls upon us
As we drift off into sleep
We hold each other through the night
This memory ours to keep.
Wykid

SWEET DREAMS

I pray you find a peaceful sleep
When you lay down your head
Find a warmth and comfort
When you crawl into bed
May your dreams be pleasant
As you slowly drift away
May the morning kiss you softly
As you begin a brand-new day.
Wykid

CAREFREE

She's standing in the kitchen
Pouring coffee in a cup
She's dancing in her nightgown
Unaware that he is up
He's watching from the hallway
She always makes him smile
In the shadows, he stays silent
And admires her for awhile
She doesn't see him behind her
He puts his hands upon her hips
She gasps from being startled
Turns toward him, kissing his lips
He brushes her hair from her eyes
His hand caressing her face
He kisses her with purpose
He loves the way her kisses taste
Holding her coffee cup in one hand
Holding her hand with the other
He leads her to the table
A new day to be discovered.
Wykid

POETRY IN MOTION

He runs his fingers over her
His poetry becomes real
The pretty pictures he painted in word
He now can touch and feel
Laying naked here before him
Responding as fingers gently graze
No fears or apprehension
She accepts the love he makes
Beauty found in silence
Breaths the only sound
Minds relaxed, yet racing
Thoughts are spinning round and round
The love they make is tender
A sweet union of two hearts
A connection of two lovers
A creation of beauty and art.
Wykid

SHOW HER

Give her your attention
Let her know she's not alone
Remind her of your own happiness
As your care for her has grown
Show her your affection
With the things you do and say
Find ways to share her smile
Kiss her softly every day
Remind her of your appreciation
Of the many things she does
Your best friend and confidant
The woman that you love.
Wykid

WALLS

We build the walls around us
To protect the heart and soul
Shielding us from showing
What others may not know
Safety found within these walls
It feels like we can breathe
A chance to reevaluate
A moment of reprieve
These walls become a prison
A sentence self-imposed
Adding to fears and loneliness
The outcome predisposed
Brick-by- brick the walls come down
The world looks fresh and new
I broke the chains, tore down my walls
The moment I met you.
Wykid

SMALL THINGS

She had a long day
Her voice relayed her stress
She is happy that it's over
She needs time to decompress
She'll be here in an hour
I set a plan in motion
To ease away her tension
With love, wine, and devotion
Grabbing several candles
And a couple of roses from a vase
A transformation of the bathroom
I start to put my plan in place
Timing is of the essence
I'm ready to begin
A bubble bath and rose petals
I wanted it perfect when she walks in
Strategically placing candles
I light them one by one
A fresh towel and her pajamas
A little music, then I'm done
I see her headlights coming
I've watched for her many times before
I pour a glass of wine for her
And I meet her at the door
I help her with her jacket
She's telling me about her day
I'm listening intently
To the things she has to say
I lead her to her favorite chair
She sits back into its clutch
Lifting her leg, I remove her boots
I enjoy this very much
She continues with her stories

While I massage her tired feet
When her story is through, I take her hand
Helping her from her seat
Leading her to the bathroom
I watch her smile when I open the door
I help her undress, folding her clothes
Neatly placing them on the floor
I excuse myself to the kitchen
Running to grab the bottle of pinot noir
I fill her glass a little too full
Then pour myself some more
The flickering of the candles
Shadows dancing on her skin
Holding my hand, she steps into the tub
I gently help her in
I sit on the floor beside her
Not speaking, I watch her relax
She leans forward and hands me a luffa
And asks me to wash her back
This time we share together
Is always special to me
I love that she allows me to care for her
Her and I become us and we.
Wykid

HIDDEN SMILES

Smiles hide a story
Laughter suppressing pain
Disguised behind happiness
Sorrows still remain
It isn't all-consuming
Yet present all the same
A broken heart, a damaged love
An emotion with no name
Unexpected tears fall
Haunting memories seem to know
The vulnerability and loneliness
Hanging on, not letting go
Smiles hide a story
A heart and love to give
Laughter shares a passion
A beautiful life to live.
Wykid

MESSAGES UNRECEIVED

Each day like the one before
Up before the sun
Following morning rituals
A new day has begun
Checking through my emails
Some for work, some of my own
Glancing over messages
Not finding it on my phone
Pouring coffee in a cup
Continuing with the mundane
Not sure what it is I'm feeling
It's not sadness, it's not pain
I guess it's disappointment
More of me than it is of you
Compounded by a loneliness
That's upsetting to me too
I may decide to write a bit
Or scribble notes on a legal pad
As reminders of what was in my head
Or the feeling that I had
Out the door, off to work
To see what adventures I can find
Though focused on the task at hand
She's always on my mind.
Wykid

WANTING

He wanted love and romance
He craved the laughter of a friend
He desired the touch of a woman
To write a story that never ends
Love notes with a hint of her perfume
A phone call just because
A random message out of the blue
Because it's him she's thinking of
He wanted to live a love story
Erotic passion written within
He wanted to give himself completely
He wanted a woman to care about him.
Wykid

THOUGHTS OF YOU

I really hope you're doing well
I thought of you today
I almost called, I wrote instead
About the things I thought I'd say
I miss the conversations
The friendly banter back and forth
The wisdom in the things you say
Keeping me on course
I saw a pretty picture
It was you that crossed my mind
I listened as a couple spoke
I thought of you in kind
I took a drive to clear my head
The results were unexpected
Rather than finding clarity
I felt more disconnected
I listened to the radio
Music is a good escape
I felt like a teenager, making a list
Of songs for a new mixed tape
Shaking my head, scolding myself
I wonder if anyone else can tell
I was thinking of you, I always do
I hope you're doing well.
Wykid

A WOMAN

The canvas of a woman
Softly touched by Heaven's brush
Comfort found within her beauty
Displaying an Angel's touch
Her eyes are so inviting
Her smile, soft and warm
Beyond wants and desires
She's more than a beautiful form
A caring love and tenderness
A spirit independent and strong
A beacon, a guiding influence
A man's direction of what is right and wrong
Without her, a man is less than
It was a woman who gave him life
A woman nurtured and cared for him
Be it, a mother, a sister, a wife
The canvas of a woman
Dimensions still unseen
Without her love, without her light
A man fails to be a King.
Wykid

CLARITY

The clouds, for me have lifted
The rain no longer falls
I'm certain storms will come again
Thank you for staying with me through it all
People have shown their kindness
My heart overflows with love
It's the singular
My friend
My person
That I am thinking of.
Wykid

EIGHT THREE ONE

She simply couldn't say it
Not in numbers
Not in words
She worried
What was he thinking
When "I Love You" remained unheard
She loved their time together
She loved his words,
Their conversations
She loved the thoughts of what the future holds
Did she love him, but with reservations?
He tried to reassure her
He was ok, he understood
Her heart will let her know when it's ok
Until then,
All is good.
Wykid

SLOWBURN

Lighting matches in the darkness
I watch them slowly burn
Mindlessly letting the thoughts creep in
Life's losses and lessons learned
Held between two fingers
Gentle flame is kissing skin
Momentary painful isolation
I strike a match again
My masochistic pleasures
Giving clarity,
Though slightly obscure
Smiling...
All the pain and lonely nights
Have brought me closer to her.
Wykid

GENTLE STROKES

A love story is written
With each deliberate stroke of a pen
Simple pleasures
A subtle romance
Falling in love all over again
With each new page that's written
As the story begins to unfold
It's her that I am thinking of
It's her I want to hold
It's her that sits beside me
While wishing upon a star
It's her who wraps her arms around me
Erasing hidden scars
I find that I am smiling
When the pen is in my hand
My words caress her softly
She's my person
I'm her man.
Wykid

SEASONS COME AND GO

The sweet taste of your kiss
Still dances on my lips
Your fragrant scent still lingers in the air
I dream and reminisce
Of your skin on fingertips
The breeze softly blowing through your hair
Jeans, torn and tattered
In this moment nothing matters
But you and I, and this moment that we share
In a blink, you're gone away
There's so much more I want to say
Am I ever going to be with you again?
Seasons come and seasons go
Like the rains and falling snows
Loneliness my only friend
Until I see you once again
Seasons come and seasons go
I just wanted you to know
As summer slowly fades away
I'd trade it all for one more day
A perfect situation
Overcome with complications
Whisper softly, don't let them hear you talk
Lock me up and hide the key
They can't know about you and me
Or the secret locked inside my heart-shaped box
In a blink, you're gone again
Another night is closing in
Without you here, I can't find the strength to sleep
The sands of time won't stop
I hear the ticking of the clock
My heart and soul are forever yours to keep
Seasons come and seasons go
I just wanted you to know
As winter slowly fades away
I'd trade it all for one more day.
Wykid

DRIFT AWAY

Hello gorgeous, it's me
How was your day?
I was thinking of you; I thought I'd send a message
I hope that it's ok
I know you're probably busy
You won't get this for a while
Just know that I am thinking of you
And that always makes me smile
If you don't have plans for dinner
I'd like to cook for you
Let you take a break
From all the things I know you do
Maybe draw you a bubble bath
A little candlelight and wine
Enjoy yourself, don't worry about me
I'll be doing fine
I can wash the dinner dishes
Maybe catch up on the news
Listen to some music
Maybe tighten your screen door screws
Take your time. Try to relax
Close your eyes and drift away
I'll be there if you need me
All you need to do is say
Let me tuck you into bed
Hold you until you sleep
I'll be there when you wake up
I am yours to keep
I better get back to work, Hon
Message me when you can
I'll be here, thinking of you
Love, your loving man.
Wykid

NATURE WALK

Will you take a walk with me?
I'd like to talk with you awhile
I want to get lost in your pretty eyes
I want to see your smile
We could walk down by the river
Where the cottonwoods provide shade
We can sit for a time if you want to
Enjoying nature's display
Or we can walk among the Aspens
Where the grass is tall and green
I know of a couple of places
That you may not have been
Maybe under the pine trees
Following game trails where they go
Discovering new destinations
Learning things we didn't know
Can I hold your hand in mine,
As our thoughts are breaking free?
I just want to spend time with you
Will you take a walk with me?
Wykid

PERFECT IMPERFECTIONS

I love the little imperfections
Tiny scars that I can trace
Each one telling a story
Of another time, another place
I watch her as she's sleeping
Listening to her breathe
Watching over and protecting her
As she travels through her dreams
Reaching out to touch her
My fingers travel her soft skin
Following the contours of her jawline
Fingertips circling her chin
I lightly kiss her bottom lip
Her sleep remains undisturbed
Propping myself up with a pillow
I continue to admire her
My eyes take in her beauty
As she lay naked in the night
I fall in love with her all over again
Loving her has always felt so right
She doesn't know I watch her
She doesn't see the woman I see
Kissing her forehead, I wish her goodnight
I'll be with her in my dreams.
Wykid

A WINDOW TO THE WORLD

A little coffee in a cup
Sunrise has cast its glow
As I'm welcoming another day
I see the world through the kitchen window
Interrupting effortless thoughts
Are dreams and memories
The things I write
The things I share
The things that no one sees
The things in life that really matter
People
Places and time
Conversations
Simple pleasures
That will forever remain mine
Moments lost
Moments shared
Moments I hope will stay
Through the darkness
I find light
I'm smiling today
Broken hearts
Broken dreams
They're not mine alone to keep
I understand
I recognize
Why others can't find sleep
I share words and poems and stories
They help me process what it is that I feel
Some are hopes
Most are my mind's creations
Wanting them to be real
With a pen and paper
I create a world for me
Beautiful pictures
Of love and romance
For all the world to see.
Wykid

ILLUSIONS

I show you what I'm thinking
I write it down in words
I tell you how I'm feeling
When my thoughts return to her
Her, is simply relative
Encompassing images in my mind
Although I love her deeply
She remains an illusion I've yet to find
A summer love
A romance
A comforting smile
A warm embrace
A friend
A partner
A confidant
A devilish mind
An Angel's face
As my thoughts are slowly fading
As her image disappears
As I close my eyes in search of sleep
Her voice whispers in my ear.
Wykid

TAKING CHANCES

She said, "I have a crush on you"
I told her, "It will pass.
I have that way with women
Nothing ever lasts."
It didn't seem to faze her
As she seduced me with her eyes
She said, "That's what I like about you
You're not like other guys."
Penetrating conversations
Foreplay in our words
Breathless from the stories
And the honesty we heard
She relinquished me of my armor
She allowed me to trust again
Tearing down the wall around my heart
I took a chance,
I let her in.
Wykid

SHARED

Will you take a walk with me?
Placing your hand in mine
Gripping my hand firmly
As our fingers intertwine
Will you share your thoughts with me?
Will you tell me about your day?
Will you share your dreams with me,
As I listen to the things you say?
Will you listen to me also?
If I have something to share—
About you and me, my life, my dreams?
Will you show me that you care?
Will you share a kiss with me—
A kiss that's soft and sweet
Romantic in its very nature
As your and my lips meet?
Will you stay the night with me?
I don't want to see you go
I know there's fear and apprehension
Of the things that you don't know
Can I see you again by chance?
I really like your company
I'll be thinking of you until then
Thank you for everything.
Signed,
Me
Wykid

UNKNOWN

Late night conversations
Genuine and real
Time to share some of the things
We love, we live, we feel
Apprehensions lifting
No expectations clouding thoughts
Some things shared in confidence
Of a life that time forgot
Smiling from out of nowhere
Anxiously awaiting each reply
Enjoying the opportunity
To discuss our reasons why
Comfort without judgment
We don't walk this world alone
It's with much appreciation
That I welcome the unknown.
Wykid

BELIEVE

Do you believe in magic,
Or perhaps in destiny?
Do miracles really happen?
Could luck reside in me?
Does love find hope in hopelessness?
Erasing painful memories
Are the lonely resurrected?
Can sorrows be set free?
Is beauty everlasting?
Can everybody see
The wonderful woman that you are?
You are beautiful to me.
Wykid

BLOWING KISSES

Kisses blown into the wind
Wishes upon a star
Hoping happiness surrounds you
No matter where you are
Little notes I write to you
For no one else to see
Hidden safely in a book
I keep them just for me
When my heart is full and happy
It's you I'm thinking of
Pen transcribes on paper
The little notes of love.
Wykid

MOTIVES

Perhaps you need to hear these words
Maybe your thoughts are tainted with doubt
You deserve to hear that someone's thinking of you
Maybe you're all they are thinking about
In a world that passes down judgment
In a world where truth is a lie
It's beautiful, feeling appreciated
Without thinking of the motives or whys
Sometimes it's really the little things
That seem to leave tracks on the heart
Embarking on a journey with someone new
Finding romance and a brand-new start
We all leave stories behind us
We all have things we regret
When someone accepts you for who you are
The past is easier to forget
We live and we learn, we become better
Or we get trapped by a life so redundant
I chose to move on and learn more about you
Where love and friendship is abundant
Don't fear the words that I scribe on a page
Don't fear when I speak about love
Love shows itself in many forms
That's the love that I'm speaking of.
Wykid

PRETTY THINGS

Today, she just feels pretty
There's a smile on her face
Her world has finally calmed a bit
Things are falling into place
She listens to her music
As she adds polish to her toes
She sings along, unashamed
To every word she knows
Wearing booty shorts and a T-shirt
She dances across the floor
Spinning and twirling, thinking of him
She's missing him once more
Maybe she'll see him this weekend
They can take a country drive
She loves the time they spend together
He makes her feel so alive.
Wykid

LOST IN THE PAGES

Flipping through the pages
Captivated by his words
Searching for the answers
The story much like hers
It's almost as if he knows her
Like he's captured her own life
The way he relates to love and romance
As well as misery and strife
She gets lost between his pages
She dreams the heroine is her
She could be his love interest
Innocent and pure
She could don a Scarlet Letter
Be the mistress he desires
The woman of his fantasies
From which his stories are inspired
Maybe she'll put down the book
Learn to know the man behind the words
Falling in love with who he is
Letting him fall in love with her.
Wykid

CONFESSIONS

Tonight, as she lay beside me
In the darkness,
I play with her hair
We talk,
I can tell she is tired
Her thoughts wandering here and there
Kissing her shoulder
No more words are spoken
Gentle fingers glide across her bare skin
Rubbing her back to the sound of her breathing
Soon,
She is sleeping again
Tracing a figure eight pattern
Across her shoulders to her waistline
Goosebumps rising along her ribcage
I notice her breathing is in cadence with mine
I begin to speak to her,
Softly
As to not awaken her from her sleep
I tell her how much I adore her
"I love you"
Three words I still keep
I almost said them once without thinking
I felt it, the words almost escaped
I caught myself
Stopped myself
Choked on the emotions
Afraid it would be a mistake
In the darkness, I felt myself smiling
Shaking my head as I replayed that day
What is the worst that could happen
If I said what I wanted to say?
Insecurities handcuff the best of us

Rejection is a realistic fear
So we stifle the thoughts
The words and ourselves
Hoping that no one will hear
As I listen to her breathing
Watching the rise and fall of each breath
I kiss her shoulder again,
And whisper "I love you"
Some things must be professed.
Wykid

HER EYES

She has a beautiful smile
But it's her eyes that speak to me
The hope, the love
The caring
The kindness she lets me see
Behind the light's reflection
The window to her soul
The scars
The pain
The sacrifices
The woman I want to know
Will I ever truly know her?
Only time will tell
Until then,
I'll admire her eyes and her smile
Always wishing her well.
Wykid

GENTLE TOUCH

He asks her to come sit with him
She sits on the floor between his thighs
Her elbows resting on his knees
He hears her as she sighs
He doesn't ask her questions
He knows she's had a long day
He'll only help to relax her
Help her stresses go away
Massaging her neck and shoulders
Kissing the top of her head
Her muscles are tense and knotted
Thank you is all that she said
He told her she was welcome
No need to say anymore
He loves that she lets him love her
He's never had this before
He isn't sure if it's for her or for him
That he does the things that he does
He's happy that he can please her
But it's his own pleasure he's thinking of
To please her is pleasing to him
Selfish in the way that he cares
His pleasure derived in making her happy
And the things she allows him to share
Little things like massages
Making dinner for her now and then
Bubble baths and candlelight
Nights out for her and her friends
Pleasing her in the bedroom
His selfishness beyond compare
He loves the way that he loves her
He loves that he brings her there
His fingers lightly massaging her temples
Small circles with a tender touch
He's happy to be sitting here with her
He loves her very much.
Wykid

SIMPLE THINGS

Holding her face between his hands
He touches her forehead with his lips
She presses her body closer to him
Her hands holding his hips
For a moment, his kiss lingers
He breathes deeply, she feels him inhale
He closes his eyes, completely content
Getting lost in her scents and smells
There's a subtle hint of her shampoo
And the perfume she likes to wear
The natural aroma of who she is
He finds entrapped in her hair
Wrapping his arms around her
Holding her tightly to him
Love is found in the simple things
Maybe this is where it begins.
Wykid

SILENT COMMUNICATION

It was more than just a kiss
There was poetry without word
Though not a word was spoken
His story could be heard
The past brought forth the present
The future was theirs to explore
A kiss with more significance
Than either could ignore
It wasn't a kiss of passion
It didn't take her breath away
It was the way that they communicated
That made her want to stay
Trust in the way he held her
His eyes were gentle and kind
It was the way he showed he cared for her
That spoke directly to her mind
Reaching to hold her hand in his
They walk quietly, side by side
The moment they shared was beautiful
Its significance cannot be denied.
Wykid

IT'S THE EYES

In her eyes, I see a kindness
A safe place to rest my gaze
Warm, soft, inviting
Getting lost in them for days
In her eyes, I see a woman
Independent, confident, and strong
Unfazed by idle judgements
Dancing to her own song
In her eyes, I see a beauty
She is beautiful for certain
Her eyes show internal beauty
Masked behind a curtain
In her eyes, I see a sadness
A sorrow caused by pain
She's been hurt but she's still standing
Standing she'll remain
In her eyes, I see the strength
Of a woman who lives her way
Not defined by another's perception
Or the trivial things people say
In her eyes, I see my reflection
I can see where changes begin
I peer behind the curtain
For an invitation to come in.
Wykid

SKELETONS

The earth is covered in a blanket of snow
The trees, left with only branches
The leaves, weeks ago falling
In the breeze, each skeleton dances
The moon is on the horizon
The sun has been nestled away
The dullness of the colors
Brings an ending to the day
Nature provides the kindling
A match producing the flame
A fire radiating its warmth
A bottle of wine is doing the same
Long into the evening
Conversations leave her empowered
Solace and serenity come
As time approaches the witching hour
A quiet mind can listen
Blinded eyes can see
There's more to learn in the darkness
Sitting among the trees.
Wykid

LESS IS MORE

Occasionally, it's the simple things
That bring about happiness
A simple drive and conversation
More derived from less
Laughing at the absurdity
Of people, place, and time
Sharing similar convictions
That in the end, we'll all be fine
Seeing different landscapes
Exploring places she's never been
Experiencing new discoveries
And the stories held within
Time goes by too quickly
When it is of concern
I could have talked for hours
There's so much more to learn
Almost as quickly as it began
It was time for it to end
Maybe there will be another chance
To spend time together again.
Wykid

FIRST KISS

The call was unexpected
She asked if she could share his time
He told her he had no objections
They could share a bottle of wine
There were romantic inclinations
With him, he wasn't sure about her
Maybe she saw him as simply a friend
Was there more? He wasn't quite sure
Those feelings were secondary
He really enjoyed her company
She seemed to understand him
With her, he could just be
He started a fire in the outdoor pit
Waiting for her to arrive
He opened the wine, pouring himself a glass
It wasn't long before she pulled into the drive
Walking over to her car to greet her
Always a gentleman, he opened her door
As she stepped out of her car, they shared a loving embrace
Like they'd done so many times before
He holds her hand as their walking
Leading her to the chairs
Listening to her as she speaks
He loves that she's willing to share
Sitting around the fire
They talk well into the night
A second bottle of wine has been opened
The moon and the stars shining bright
Uncertain if it's the wine he hears speaking
But his feelings can't be dismissed
He leans in a little bit closer
Tonight they share their first kiss.
Wykid

THE GAZE

Painted toes and toe rings
A pedicure in recent days
The fading colors of a rose tattoo
Ankle bracelet with dolphins and waves
Her legs are tan and silky smooth
Her skirt doesn't cover her sculpted thighs
Crossed, like a lady, as she sits in the chair
Her beautiful legs have caught my eye
Her skirt is black and pleated
Her blouse, a sleeveless shade of white
Three buttons left unfastened
Form-fitting, but not too tight
I notice a couple of bracelets
A thumb ring on her left hand
A few more rings on her fingers
No evidence of a wedding band
White wine at her table
She sips from a near empty glass
Her smile is intoxicating
I'm listening to her laugh
A small gathering of beautiful ladies
She's obviously in good company
I'm sitting alone, just watching
Enjoying the beauty I see
Another bottle of wine has been opened
Their good times not ready to end
Occasionally, she laughs until she cries
In her conversations with friends
Wine slowly passing between her lips
Her eyes connecting with mine
I don't blink, I can't look away
I seem to be frozen in time
I see the crease of her subtle smile

Shyly, she unlocks her gaze
Looking back, she gives me a second glance
I'm caught, still looking her way
I give her a courteous tip of my hat
As I return her smile
She doesn't seem to mind that I'm watching her
So I'll be sitting here for a while.
Wykid .

MY LOVES

I love the smell of sage in bloom
The smells of dirt and pines in the spring
I love the scent of Aspen leaves
I love the song that the Meadowlark sings
I love the sound of a bulging elk
I follow trails where they lead
I love sitting alone on a mountain top
The only religion that I need
I love the laughter of a woman
I love the innocence of a child
I love living in Wyoming
Going where she's still rugged and wild
I love the touch of a woman's skin
I love conversations, meaningful and deep
I love listening as a woman describes her day
I love watching her as she sleeps
I love summer nights at the cabin
I love rebuilding my father's dream
I love baiting bears with my daughter
Sharing the things that we've seen
I love that I can find happiness
Through the hardships and chaos I've known
I love my kids and my granddaughter
Thankful to see how they've grown
When I lay my head on my pillow
I'm content with the life that I live
I appreciate the things that I have
I'm happy with the love that I give.
Wykid

SECRET TOUCH

I can't touch her in the literal sense
She doesn't know the secret I hide
It's best that I don't tell her
It's best to keep my feelings inside
Maybe I can caress her mind
With words derived from thought
Painting a picture of what I see in her
The things I see, that she cannot
Perhaps her heart will notice
Beating stronger, keeping pace
Filling her with a happiness
Putting a smile on her face
Will laughter break the silence,
Suppressing apprehension she may hold?
Will she find my humor comforting?
Will the layers begin to unfold?
Will her dreams allow me to enter?
Will we walk on common ground?
Will daydreams catch her thinking of me
When there's no one else around?
Wykid

A PENNY FOR YOUR THOUGHTS

A penny for your thoughts
A nickel for your dreams
A quarter for your story
The ups and downs
The in-betweens
There is no price tag on true happiness
True riches are found in love
That is the you I am wanting to know—
The you that I'm thinking of
I see the stars on a cloudless night
I wonder,
Are you seeing them too?
When questions arise and I'm seeking direction
I ask myself,
"What would she do?"
I enjoy our time together
I carry you with me throughout my days
Smiling,
Embracing the feeling
Hoping that it always stays
Tonight,
As I sit in a forest
With the lions, the wolves, and the bears
I reflect on my own life and story
The parts of it that I share
Memories are what dreams are made of
The things we remember
The times we forgot
I close my eyes so that I can see you
A penny for your thoughts.
Wykid

A WANTING

I want to know your imperfections
I want to see your scars
I want to watch you,
While you're not aware
Simply being who you are
I want to hear your craziest stories
I want to listen to your dreams
I want to share your smile,
Hear your laughter,
Feel the comfort that they bring
I want to listen to your voice
On the other end of the line
I want to hear about your hectic day
As you let yourself unwind
I want to help you when you need me
I want to support you where I can
I want to be the one you can depend on
As a lover, a friend, and a man
I want to be selfish in the way I care
In the ways I let it show
My pleasures come by pleasing you
It's the only way I know.
Wykid

PERFECTION

I paint her from the perfect canvas
Every curve and every line
Every thought and every image
Carefully created in my mind.
Wykid

WHISPERS IN THE WIND

Listen…
Hear the silence
The whispers in the wind
The calming of the chaos
Serenity seeping in
Listen…
Hear her heartbeat
The things she doesn't say
A look
A smile
Speaking volumes
Where words get in the way
Listen…
Hear the music
The crescendo's rise and fade
Touch her with intention
Feel the rhythm of love that's being made
Listen…
Hear her breathing
The sound of peaceful sleep
Hold her closely
In your arms
Your love is hers to keep.
Wykid

THINKING OF YOU

When I think of you
The grass is green
The air is warm and light
Shadows dance on fields of flowers
Nighttime skies are starlit and bright
When I think of you
I see crystal clear waters
A mountain lake
A meandering stream
A cabin in peaceful seclusion
A calming, therapeutic scene
When I think of you
The radio's playing
A two-track road
A canopy of trees
Bare feet rest on the dashboard
Hands resting upon naked knees
When I think of you
The leaves have changed color
An anticipated chill in the air
Summer shorts and sandals
Giving way to fall fashions
A new wardrobe?
A new perfume?
New hair?
When I think of you
I see the world in a blanket
A cocoon of fresh fallen snow
Untracked
Undisturbed
Pure in its presence
Like the winters I knew long ago
When I think of you

I see your smile
I see your eyes
So caring and kind
I see your hands
I see the stories that they tell
As my fingers and yours intertwine
When I think of you
The sun's sitting higher
Slowly climbing in the warming Spring sky
New changes
Bring about new beginnings
Like the ones that I see for you and I
When I think of you
Time keeps on ticking
Each passing day provides a memory or two
Though,
It's all in my mind and the visions I dream of
That's what I see when I'm thinking of you.
Wykid

SUBTLE FLAMES

A gentle touch
A soft caress
Fingers touching skin
Careless whispers
Burning passions
Fires that burn within
Primal secrets
Left untold
Desires remain forbidden
Cloaked behind the innocence
Of that which remains hidden
Suppressing the desires
Lost in time and place
Resurrecting deeper feelings
That time cannot erase
As my head lays on the pillow
Lights are turned down low
I hope that my dreams take me
To a place that we both know.
Wykid

LOSING SIGHT

The morning found him melancholy
Trying to make sense
Staring at his coffee cup
Viewing life in the past tense
Many good years behind him
Do the best years lie ahead?
He shakes his head,
Mumbling curses
Thinking of the things he wished he'd said
Living for the moment
Soaking in the now
Losing sight of what he really wanted
Letting it slip away somehow
The slightest crease of a smile
As he starts to reminisce
The sunset around the fire
Peach Crown
And the first kiss.
Wykid

I SEE HER

Some might see her scars
I see the battles won
Some might see her sadness
I see the things she's overcome
Some might see her aging,
A few wrinkles, graying hair
I see a wife,
A mother
Giving all she has to share
Some might see her broken heart
I see her try to mend
Some might question, selfishly
I see a selfless friend
Some might misunderstand her
Some might judge the path she chose
As for me,
I think she's beautiful
I wonder if she knows.
Wykid

VICES

With the burning of a 1000 suns
Passion found a vein
Intensity unbridled
Desires uncontained
Hopelessly addicted
Nothing could suffice
It was her all along
She is his favorite vice.
Wykid

TIME

It is your time that I am craving
It is your kiss, your taste, your touch
It is your voice, your words, your laughter
Your smiling eyes that mean so much
There are things I want to tell you
There is so much I want to say
But the unknowns keep me silent
When my own words get in the way
I wanted only to hold you
Taking your hand in mine
Walk with you
Talk with you
Losing track of time
Your kisses... they do melt me
Leaving me wanting more
Every taste of you on my lips
Is better than before
Time...
I hope we find some
Just you and I
With nowhere to be
Sharing with me things I don't know
As I share the same of me
Desire is undeniable
I want to touch you and taste your skin
Sharing my passion with you
Over and over again
I want to feel your heartbeat
Lying beside you,
Your head on my chest
Fingertips lightly touching your skin
Until you slip into a peaceful rest
The story just beginning

A blank canvas on every page
Waiting to be written
A romance now uncaged.
Wykid

STORIES UNWRITTEN

Scribing the words with purpose
Thoughts illicit the dreams
Fantasy formed by reality
Though, nothing is quite as it seems
For instance,
Let me show you a woman
With the passion of life in her eyes
Beautiful
Fun
Engaging
Yet, I don't see the nights that she cries
There is a man who looks into the mirror
He wonders,
What does the world see?
Does it see him the way that he sees himself
Battling his own doubts and insecurities
The picture changes course and direction
As I write it,
The romance comes alive
Stealing a kiss
Touching her face
Two people just trying to survive
Together, the days bring the smiles
The nights hold the secrets they share
A story unwritten
Waiting for the words
Painting a new love affair.
Wykid

EVERYTHING AND NOTHING

He kissed her forehead and rubbed her shoulder
"Hey you, are you alive?"
...I don't think so, what time is it?
"It's a little after five..."
...Ugh, why are you waking me?
Lay down, come back to bed...
Her breathing stopped,
Eyes welling up with tears
When she listened to what he said...
"Last night, I watched you as you were sleeping
I fell in love with you all over again.
I've always loved you,
Last night was different
I'm not sure where to begin.
It's everything
It's nothing
I simply love you for you being you
The chaos
The craziness
The ups and the downs
The goofy things that you do.
I thought about life
Our different paths
How after all of these years
Our lives merged together.
The years that I've missed
All the while loving you
Thinking I'd be without you forever.
A random act of kindness
You always did give so selflessly
The smallest of sparks igniting a fire
Knowing that you were thinking of me.
I listened to you breathing

Watching the rise and fall of your chest
Kissing you softly,
So as not to disturb you
That's when I got up and left.
I walked outside and looked to the heavens
There were a million stars in the sky
I made a wish upon a shooting star
Then a single teardrop fell from my eye
Overcome with emotions
Why?
I can't really explain
Thankful for you
Sad for your sorrows
Wishing that I could bear your burden of pain
I'm not sure how long I stood there
A couple of hours,
Maybe a little more
Thinking about you
Thinking about love
Thinking about the life that you knew before
I noticed the light slowly changing
A new morning soon to be seen
I was hoping that maybe you'd like to see it—
Sharing this sunrise with me."
Wykid

WELCOMING THE STORM

She came upon me slowly
Like a beautiful midsummer storm
Building on the horizon
Comforting and warm
Echoes of distant thunder
Long before seeing the flashing of light
A calmness overtaking me
A prelude to the night...
She...
She exemplifies beauty
Vibrant
With a passion for life
A wonderful mother
An entrusted friend
A daughter
A sister
A wife
The storms that we find bring uncertainty
Unknown are the paths we discover
In the winds and the rains
In the seasons that change
We find life
In a friend and a "lover"...
Memories made last a lifetime
The heart holding them tender and dear
Irreplaceable in their true meaning
Everlasting
With each passing year...
I watch the clouds as they're building
Anticipating the storms they may bring
Trusting in their natural beauty
Welcoming them,
I embrace everything

The storms of the past, a reminder
I need to say what I'm wanting to say
There is no right or wrong in the way that I'm feeling
I thought she was beautiful today.
Wykid

LINGERING

We talked,
It seemed for hours
As I ran my fingers through her hair
I listened to her every word
And the things she chose to share
Some moments found us laughing
Some moments stopping time
She shared with me her hopes and dreams
In turn, I told her mine
I found a smile in the mirror
She is with me, even when I'm alone
I could smell her perfume
Hear the sound of her voice
As I was finding my way back home.
Wykid

MISSING

Talk to me
Tell me a story
I'd like to hear the things you have to say
How did you sleep?
Did you catch the sunrise?
What adventures await you today?
Missing you hasn't been easy
I couldn't have known that I'd miss you this much
The sound of your voice
Your smile
Your eyes
Your kiss
Your embrace
And your touch
Some days I feel like a kid again
Discovering the world brand new
Talk to me
Tell me a story
I want to know more about you.
Wykid

UNSENT

I wrote it
I couldn't send it
Although every word is true
Life and love
New beginnings
The way I feel about you
It frightened me
The thoughts I shared
Reading them fully exposed
Not knowing if you'd understand
The message I composed.
Wykid

I WANTED YOU

I wanted to hold your hand
I was afraid you'd pull away
I wanted to tell you the way that I feel
Afraid you wouldn't hear what I was trying to say
I wanted to hold your face in my hands
Kissing your lips
Breathing you in
I wanted to look into your eyes
Losing myself in them again
I wanted to give you the space and the time
Patient in what I say and do
I wanted these things
And so much more
I wanted to be lying next to you...
Wykid

ANTICIPATION

With each turn of the page
A story unfolding
Anticipating the next spoken word
Closing my eyes
So that I can see clearly
The message that I should have heard
I hear,
But, I'm not sure that I listen
I listen,
But, I'm not sure that I hear
Suppressing the sad and the painful
Ignorance cultivated by fear
For a moment,
The world's right and perfect
Her fingers interlaced with my own
Comforted by her scent and her presence
It's in her arms that I feel like I'm home
My eyes open,
I can still see her
The distance doesn't obstruct my view
The stories I write
The pictures I'm painting
Are pleasant reminders of you.
Wykid

REMINDED

I needed just a little while
Another moment of your time
A chance to say what I didn't say
Ever present in my mind
Hellos come and go so quickly
Goodbyes linger long after you're gone
Reminders come in many forms
Places, pictures, and songs
The missing...
Echoes of emptiness
All of the things that I should have said
Replaying the time we spent together
Movies playing inside my head
I smile whenever I think of you
I think of you more than you know
I needed just a little while
Before you had to go.
Wykid

ONE FOUR THREE

"I love you"
Such a simple statement
Eight letters
Three words
One meaning
Capturing what my heart's telling me
Harnessing the feeling
Foreign to me for many years
Uncertainty in how to proceed
I trip and I stumble
I slip and fall
Confused by my wants and my needs
143
A beautiful arrangement
Conveying my message to you
I see you in each morning sunrise
You're in the sunsets
When each day is through
A perfectly simple arrangement
Letters and numbers
I find on my phone
459 translates as ILY
I can't wait until you come back home.
Wykid

RYLEE JAMES

Let me take a moment
A couple of minutes to explain
How it is that I find happiness
Amidst the sadness and the pain
It took my own reflections
How did I get here?
It's the love that's lived inside me
For six months and twenty years
I struggle with the sadness
I wish I had done more
It's the memories of the laughter
Of the time we had before
As the sadness washes over me
A happiness is found
Love finds me when I least expect it
Good fortunes abound
My kids, my girls, my strength, and hope
They help me to stand strong
With me
Right beside me
Is where they all belong
Love notes and conversations
Late into the night
Good night
Good morning
143
Makes everything alright.
Wykid

SHE DOESN'T KNOW

Bare feet curled up beneath her
Pillows propped up on the couch
Denim jeans with rolled up cuffs
A burgundy-colored blouse
Eyeglasses adorn her face
Long hair is free and flowing
I watch her from across the room
She has no way of knowing…
She doesn't know the happiness
The pride
The love
The caring
She doesn't know the deeper passions
From the time that we are sharing
She couldn't know the hidden fears
Although, I've shared a few
Or that she makes me a better me
Sometimes I wish she knew
I love her,
Far beyond the words
I know that she's afraid
I hope she feels it in my touch
And in the love that we have made
I'm thankful that she's in my life
I truly enjoy her company
I miss her in times that we're apart
She is beautiful to me.
Wykid

SPACES IN BETWEEN

It's not the dates that define the life
It's the spaces in between
Only those who know love and loss
Understand just what that means
My life is complicated
But simple just the same
I love without condition
But conditions still remain
Those who came before me
Those who possess a familiar name
I'm good
I'm happy
My life content
I appreciate the life I know
I only wish that I could share
The love I want to show
Nothing has prepared me
For world that now exists
The wanting
The needing
The romance
That was shared in our first kiss.
Wykid

LONGING

I thought of her today
But hell,
Most days I do
She's in my thoughts
She's in my dreams
I wondered
If she was thinking of me too
I wanted to call her number
I wanted to hear her voice
I wanted to tell her how I feel
But I don't really have a choice
Sometimes I push the envelope
Sometimes it just slips out
831
143
She knows what I'm talking about
I want her here beside me
I want to be where she is now
I want to tell her that I love her
I want to prove my love somehow.
Wykid

SHE'S HOME

It's a 1000 things
And then some
That make her feel like home
True grit wrapped in sophistication
She's unlike any woman I have known
I can't help but smile
As I navigate my day
I can't wait to hear her voice
Listening to the things she has to say
Her eyes
Her smile
Her laughter
Her intelligence, style, and grace
Her beauty resides within her
Still, I'm drawn to her pretty face
I find that I am thankful
For the time we get to share
She's stood beside me through the storms
Hand in hand
I know she cares
Me
Wykid

LITTLE INDENTATIONS

The indentation on the paper
Left a simple "I Love You"
A tell-tale sign of a note now written
The words were showing through
A little yellow notepad
A simple ballpoint pen
Where he wrote his thoughts
Where he captured feelings
To be revisited now and then
She ran her finger across the letters
She whispered them quietly
She said the words,
It made her smile
"I think he really loves me…"
He wonders if she saw it
The note he left for her
If she did,
Did she keep it or throw it away
He has no way of knowing for sure
It's that little yellow notepad
With that simple ballpoint pen
Sitting right beside him
As he's writing down thoughts again.
Wykid

PAINTING PICTURES

She is a paint-by-color portrait
A vision of the picture I see
Capturing the very essence
Of who I imagine her to be
Eyes revealing a kindness
A smile inviting and warm
Hair that dances in the moonlight
Her voice,
A calm in the storm
Her touch,
Both, exciting and soothing
Igniting fires
With a sensual flame
Bringing peaceful tranquility
When it's needed the most
Always, without judgment or blame
Nurturing and compassionate
Passionate in the dark of the night
Adventurous in our journey
Encouraging the things that I write
The picture is slowly fading
Erased as I put down my pen
I hope to repaint her image
Goodnight and goodbye until then.
Wykid

CASTLES IN THE SAND

Building castles
Writing love notes
Drawing hearts in the sand
Watching waves come ever closer
Washing them all away again
People come and people go
Some stay to weather the storms
Sharing laughter
Sharing tears
Loving arms to keep you warm
Some,
Like me
Rebuild the castles
Love notes become poems
Dreaming of my minds illusions
Where romance finds a home.
Wykid

DISCOVERIES

Her intelligence intrigues me
She has a beautiful mind
Attractiveness compounded
By each new discovery I find
Thought-provoking challenges
Unveiling layers of who I am
Teaching me
While guiding me
Through things I didn't understand
It's in the conversations
I find it in her words
The beauty and admiration
I see when I think of her.
Wykid

SEIZE THE MOMENTS

To love... and to be loved
Simple pleasures that seize the day
Moments providing happiness
We carry with us along the way
Navigating the roughest of waters
Headstrong into the storms
Knowing that they too will pass
We'll see the sun and feel its warmth
It's a journey we embark on
Not a destination or place
Seen in the eyes and the smile
And in the way the light kisses their face
Seeking another's energy
Feeling it deep within
Cradled in the comfort
Of touching, skin to skin
Trusting the emotions
Devotion, unquestioned and pure
Hand in hand,
Walking together
A love that will endure.
Wykid

TELL ME

Come sit with me a moment
I'd like to hear about your day
Rest your head upon my shoulder
As I listen to what you say
Tell me about your morning
Did you awake with the sunrise?
Or did the day allow for extra sleep
Before you opened your pretty eyes?
Did you enjoy a cup of coffee,
Or maybe a cup of tea?
Did you take some time,
For yourself
Before embarking on the day's journey?
What did you discover
As the clock erased past time?
Were you able to find the joys and comfort
That stimulate your mind?
My apologies for all of the questions
I'll be quiet now,
Until you are through
I can't help myself
I want to know
Everything about you.
Wykid

SPELLBOUND

She doesn't see what my eyes see
When I look into her eyes
The beauty that she radiates
Where her truth and passion lies
Her smile captives me
Eliciting my own
Getting lost in thought
Lost in emotions
Her mysteries unknown
She doesn't feel my heartbeat
The warmth that rushes through my veins
The excitement and the anxiousness
At the mention of her name
I don't understand it
I try to rationalize what I see
Spellbound by her image
She is beautiful to me.
Wykid

DEPTHS

Depth of thought and depth of feeling
Emotions raw and pure
Deeper trust and understanding
When my mind reflects on her
It wasn't by intention
It wasn't by design
The natural progression
The sequence of place and time
In a world so vast and unknown
I can only watch as it unfolds
Embracing new beginnings
And stories yet to be told.
Wykid

COOLER WEATHER

When the leaves have all changed colors
When they're lying on the ground
When the skies give way to winter
When snowflakes fall without a sound
When the morning frosts are heavy
When the nights beckon a fire
When the whiskey courses through my veins
It's still you that I desire
When days have become shorter
When the darkness lingers on
When the Northern winds are blowing
I'll be listening to her song
When the winter chill is biting
When the cold is getting through
I feel a warmth that settles over me
When I stop to think of you.
Wykid

A GENTLEMAN'S PRAYER

I pray that morning comes to you gently
I wish I didn't have to leave
I'd love to lay here next to you
To hold you as you sleep
May the sunlight sparkle in your eyes
And softly kiss your skin
Know I'm thinking of you
Until I'm here with you again.
Wykid

CAMP PENDLETON

The desert meets the ocean
The waves come crashing in
Where one lifetime has ended
Another is ready to begin
Walking the edge of a razor
Between happiness and despair
Letting go
While holding on
To what is gone and what's still there
I don't deny reality
Yet I stand in disbelief
How can I be so happy
When I'm filled with so much grief?
A puzzle has many pieces
I have to find the ones that fit
I know that one is missing
There is no replacing it
As pieces slowly fit together
The picture coming into view
I'm finding peace
I'm finding comfort
I owe it all to you.
Wykid

SUMMER DAZE

She kicks off her summer sandals
To feel the cool grass beneath her feet
Drinks on ice
Friends gathered together
Enjoying the midday heat
Laughter, games, and conversation
A perfect summer day
Sitting around a fire
As the sun slowly fades away
Lightning flashes in the Western sky
The sound of thunder rolls
Drops of rain
A summer breeze
Soothing to her soul
I can see the picture
Crystal clear
She sits in the shadows of flickering light
Dancing flames
Seemingly kissing her skin
Under the stars tonight
I watch from where I'm sitting
I feel like I'm a million miles away
Silently, not saying a word
Only wishing I could stay.
Wykid

MY WILD ROSE

A rose is insignificant
When blooming in the wild, alone
Its beauty going unnoticed
A simple flower guarded by thorns
When discovered by an attentive eye
It stands insignificant no longer
Complex and beautiful
Its appeal is growing stronger
When I look at the rose
I'm reminded of a woman
She carries these qualities too
Beautiful,
Even when standing alone
I share this rose with you.
Wykid

CHANGING LANDSCAPES

The crashing of the waves
A constant, steady force
Carving out the landscape
Predictable in its course
We watch,
But we don't question
What will be will be
One by one
Waves come rushing in
Gently return to the sea
Today I felt the waves of change
A rising of the tide
The whisper of a new direction
Echoing inside
I welcome the discovery
Seeing the world brand new
The changing of the ebb and flow
Have brought me here to you.
Wykid

WYOMING WOMAN

Wyoming's stars shine brighter
When reflecting in a woman's eyes
The fire burns a little warmer
With a woman by your side
The Aspens and the pine trees
Seem to take on a different view
Nature feels more natural
When a woman shares it with you
The waters of a mountain stream
Have never looked so crystal clear
The high peaks of the Gros Ventre mountains
More majestic when she's near
The silence shared together
Speaking loudly to the heart
The world is less inspiring
When two souls must be apart.
Wykid

SEEING IS BELIEVING

She doesn't see what I see
She doesn't believe the things I say
She doesn't know she's beautiful
But I tell her anyway
Her legs are lying across my lap
Barefoot,
With painted toes
I smile as I rub them
I don't think she really knows
I'm not supposed to say it
So I try to suppress the way I feel
No matter how hard I try though
I know what I'm feeling is real
I love her for the woman she is
The friend that she's been to me
I love her for being my person
There's so much to her that she doesn't see.
Wykid

INTERJECTION

I wrote myself into the picture
It's where I wanted to be
I created my own novel
To be read by only me
In the turning of the pages
I discovered the unknown
There is more of me I've yet to give
More of me yet to be shown
The lover and the fighter
A man of finite words
Though when I share
I share in verses
Maybe then my words are heard
Giving without limits
When affection is returned
Sometimes crawling deep into my cave
Licking wounds from lessons learned
Observing those around me
Thinking I may be flawed or broken
But their superficial happiness
Is exposed when words are spoken
I realized that we're all different
But we are also all the same
Seeking love and happiness
Guarded from past pain
With each stroke of the pen and the pencil
Exposing the world that I see
My personal novel
My personal story
Of a love that resides inside of me.
Wykid

GETTING TO KNOW HER

I want to know her chaos
I want to learn her fears
I want to see her when she's vulnerable
I want to wipe away her tears
I want to share dances in the kitchen
I want to listen to her sing
I want to see her when she's happy
I want to know the joy it brings
I want coffee for two at the kitchen table
I want to have dinners and candlelight
I want to sit with her as she bathes
I want to talk with her each night
I want to walk my fingers down her spine
I want to rub her back as she falls asleep
I want be with her in her dreams
I want to be hers to keep.
Wykid

DINNER FOR TWO

He's busy in the kitchen
Checking the clock
He has plenty of time
Making chicken and sausage
Over penne pasta
He pours a glass of wine
Feeling content
He's happy
Humming and singing a song
Dancing alone
Knowing no one is watching
She's on her way
It shouldn't be long
Place settings on the table
Two candles on the centerpiece
Linen napkins, burgundy red
Holding a perfect crease
He hears her pull into the driveway
Greeting her at the door
He kisses her cheek, she smiles
Kissing him back once more
Wine in her glass
He asks her to sit
She shares the events of her day
Pasta now strained,
He serves up two plates
In the background she hears music play
Turning down the lights
The candles now flicker,
Casting a romantic glow
Across the table from her
A man who adores her
Someone she's thankful to know.

Wykid

MUSIC AND LYRICS

The rhythm of love
Silence now broken
Harmonic waves
In love's language when spoken
Three-quarter time
Count and beats measured
Lyrically painting
A picture that's treasured
Heartbeat and tempo
A song to be sung
You and I walking
To the beat of our drum.
Wykid

FEELING BEAUTIFUL

She only needs a little while
A half an hour,
Maybe more
To lose herself
To find herself
Behind the bathroom door
The water slowly rising
The bubbles start to form
She feels the tension easing
As she anticipates the warmth
She begins undressing
Her clothes discarded on the floor
She pauses,
Looking into the mirror
Where is the girl she knew before
Age has graced her kindly
In both figure and in form
A few gray hairs
A few new wrinkles
A few scars of a life well worn
Smiling as she turns away
She is happy,
Everything is okay
Some battles just aren't worth the fight
She feels beautiful today.
Wykid

MEASURING TIME

Measured in minutes
In hours
In days
The second hand ticking
As time passes away
The greatest gift that we have to give
Time shared with another
Life treasured
Life lived
We don't get time back
It's our own conscious gift
To spend and to choose
Who we will share it with
Precious moments
Precious memories
In the sharing of time
It's time shared with you
That enhances mine.
Wykid

LOVE NOTES

I left a love note by your pillow
And another by your coffee cup
I didn't want to wake you
Maybe you'll find them when you get up
I left you at least a dozen
Before I headed out the door
Don't worry if you don't find them all
I'll write you 1000 more
Xs n Os.
Wykid

PICTURES IN THE DARK

Random patterns and figure eights
Fingers lightly touching your skin
Stopping at your panty line
Then starting all over again
Hearts and letters
Pictures and words
Love notes to you from me
Erasing them all with the palm of my hand
The pictures and words that I see
It's only my imagination
The images filtering through
Smiling in the darkness
I woke up thinking of you.
Wykid

MOMENTS SHARED

She only shares of herself with you
What she wants you to see
The most precious thing she has is her time
I wish she'd share her time with me
She's most vulnerable when she's intimate
There's risk in her letting go
Value her trust
Trust her values
And the honesty she shows
When you love her
Love her completely
Appreciate the woman
The body
The mind
Discover the woman you've found in her
Explore the treasures that you find
Think of her in her absence
Hold her closely when night comes to call
Walk beside her
Hand in hand
Catch her when she falls
She only shares of herself with you
The things that she wants you to see
The most precious thing she has is her time
I wish she'd share her time with me.
Wykid

MORE THAN YOU KNOW

You are more than what your eyes see
You are more than what you fear
You are more than how you view yourself
When you look into the mirror
You are more than all of your failures
You are more than your success
You are more than the images in your mind
You are more than the sins that you confess
You are more than the words that reach your ears
You are more than another's view
There is more to you than you let show
There is so much more to you.
Wykid

MESSAGES

Leaving little love notes
Just to say the things I want to say
Subtle little reminders
That I think of her everyday
A note left on the pillow
A card next to her coffee cup
A rose left on the bathroom vanity
To greet her when she gets up
"I love you" on the mirror
Written with a finger, but she can't see
Until the steam from her morning shower
Shows the message left by me
Sometimes it's the little things
Sometimes a simple touch will do
Sometimes I simply sit and watch
Falling madly in love with you.
Wykid

EMBRACING THE DAY

It's the realness that's most beautiful
The pureness of emotion
The messy hair
No makeup, no gown
A mind of chaos and commotion
An occasional tear of sadness
Cursing out of frustration
Learning what it is she needs
Without words, without translation
This is the woman behind the face
Behind the confidence she portrays
A woman who takes life as it comes
Knowing we all have shitty days
Her hands, occasionally dirty
Hard work, not foreign to her
At the end of the day
She finds pride in herself
Her heart is kind and pure
I find her intelligence attractive
Her opinions help reshape my own
Her presence calming the roughest of waters
Her embrace, it feels like home.
Wykid

A LOVE THAT FITS LIKE THAT

A pair of leather work gloves on the dashboard
Worn in, a perfect mold
I want a love that fits like that
A woman's hand that I can hold
My dusty pair of Georgia Boots
My dirty, sweat-stained cowboy hat
Comfortable and reliable
I want a love that fits like that
The wheels hum on the highway
White line guides me on my right
I don't have a love like that
There's no one waiting for me tonight
A left turn onto a dirt road
A few more miles and I'll be home
There's no light on to welcome me
Another night I'll spend alone
I crack the top off of a cold beer
I hang my hat up on its rack
Content in the walls that surround me
Looking forward, never back
It's just me and my Blue Heeler
I tell him about my day
I see love and loyalty in his eyes
I want a love that looks at me that way.
Wykid

UNCOMFORTABLY COMFORTABLE

I love the way it feels
Yet, it's uncomfortable
I love the way my thoughts lose track of time
When one thought has run its unpredictable course
A new one finds its way into my mind
An ice-laden pool
The trickling sound of water
Snow as it crunches under feet
Bring to me thoughts of fields of flowers
You and I in the warm summer heat
Windows down
Bare feet on the dash
Music, conversations, and smiles
Nowhere to go
No place to be
New discoveries with each passing mile
Fading like the setting sun
A new vision comes into view
Dinner for two
You look stunning tonight
I love your hair
Your dress
And your shoes
I stand a little taller
Confident
Refind
I can't hear what we're saying
But you are smiling at me
Before vanishing from my mind
A lazy Sunday morning
Pillows hearing everything we say
Sharing
Laughing

Touching
And talking
Before we start the day
Uncomfortable with the projections
Yet, unwilling to let them go
Painting a perfect love affair
With someone I'm wanting to know.
Wykid

DON'T LET HER KNOW

Shhhh,
Don't let her hear you
Don't let your words get in the way
It's ok for you to think it
But somethings you just can't say
Whisper what you're feeling
Tell it to the gentle winds
Maybe you can write it down
When the thoughts are rushing in
She can't know you thought about her
When you saw a couple holding hands
Or that you miss her in her absence
I'm not sure she'd understand
When the beauty of a moment
Or a picture catches your eye
Let the image capture you
Before it passes by
See her in the sunsets
Find her by an alpine lake
Bare feet soaking in a stream
Watch her sleep when you're awake
Walk with her in a field of flowers
Run your fingers through her hair
Kiss her forehead
Paint her toes
It's ok for you to care
Talk with her
But listen
Value the time she spends with you
Think of her
Share your dreams
The way that lovers do
Shhhh,

Don't let her hear you
Somethings you just can't say
Let your heart speak for you
When you think of her today.
Wykid

A SPLENDID EVENING

The crackling of the fire
Smoke floating on the mountain air
The sun is slowly setting
Birds are roosting here and there
The steady sound of water
From a stream not far below
Shadows slowly dancing
In the sunset's dying glow
Two chairs around the fire
One for you and one for me
Reflecting on the moment
Thankful for the beauty that I see
Resting your feet upon my lap
You talk about the day
Listening to the sound of your voice
And the things you have to say
A picture-perfect memory
Captured in the mountain air
Stirring the fire, I smile
Wishing you were really there.
Wykid

COME WITH ME

Come a little closer
I want to whisper in your ear
You look exceptionally beautiful tonight
I can't wait to get you out of here
Do you think anyone will miss us?
It's only half past nine
Follow me,
Let's take a walk
Put your hand in mine
I know a place that we can go
Where we can be alone
I don't want to share you tonight
I want you for my own
Let's sit by the water's edge
We can watch the sun as it sets tonight
Let me put my arms around you
I want to hold you tight
I love the perfume you're wearing
I think you've worn that one before
Your smile...
Your smile is melting me
Making me want you more
Thank you for sharing your night with me
It's these moments that I miss
Where we can talk, and laugh together
I'm really enjoying this...
Wykid

ONCE JADED

It's the meaningful conversations
Late into the night
Sharing thoughts and feelings
Knowing she'll help me do what's right
Giving trust completely
Being trusted just the same
Smiling with my heart and soul
Each time she calls my name
Intimacy and romance
Love and lust abound
Missing her completely
In the times she's not around
Listening to her heartbeat
Touching her tender skin
Watching her as she's sleeping
Falling in love all over again
A few of the things that I'm missing
As I travel these roads alone
A woman compliments a man
She makes a house a home
My mind has not forgotten
Though my heart has long turned cold
To the thought of sharing my life with someone
Holding hands as we grow old.
Wykid

HOLDING ON AND LETTING GO

I noticed there was something different
She had a familiar glow
I remember when she shared it with me
But that was long ago
I love to see her happy
Yet, it saddens me to see
Her newfound happiness with someone else
When she used to find it with me
I don't know when it slipped away
Putting distances between us
A wedge driving ever deeper
In our loyalty and trust
My heart says keep on fighting
Try to win her over again
My love for her says let her go
She has fallen in love with him.
Wykid

DAY BY DAY

Where does time go?
The years slowly fade away
The hourglass depleting
Moment by moment, day by day
Where does love go?
When it can no longer be found
The one you loved is gone
Alone
There is no one else around
Life goes on without you
When you're lying on the floor
Tears are falling down
And you just can't take it anymore
The world keeps on spinning
The sun will rise another day
A new love is waiting for you
Don't let it slip away
Time has made you stronger
Wisdom gained beyond the years
The love you want is waiting
If you cast away your fears
The world will bring new love to you
The heart will guide the way
A beautiful life to share together
Let that love shine on you today.
Wykid

MEMORIES

Some memories last a lifetime
Some drift away in the wind
Here today
Gone tomorrow
Never to be visited again
I hold onto my memories
Never letting go
Sharing them
With those I love
The things they didn't know
Every little detail
Every image crystal clear
The simple and the profound
Staying with me through the years
New memories and new beginnings
Pretty pictures of the past
Safely held inside my mind
I know they'll always last.
Wykid

SIMPLE TIMES

Do you ever miss the simplicity
Of holding hands and taking a walk?
Smiling for all the right reasons
A time to listen, a time to talk?
Living in the moment
With nowhere else that you'd rather be?
These are the things that cross my mind
When I think about you and me
Do you ever wish that time would stand still?
That a moment would never pass
A kiss, a touch, or a memory
A night that would forever last?
Forever comes with a timestamp
Memories are a life lived before
Reminders of an expired time and place
That don't exist anymore
Further removed as each day passes
Fading are the hopes and the dreams
The path becoming more isolated
The only constant is a lonely theme.
Wykid

STRANGERS IN THE NIGHT

There were no words
Not even a whisper
Like strangers passing in the night
I don't think I even noticed
Until long after we passed by
Mystic solidarity
A soul's unification
Comfortable familiarity
Silent in communication
Suddenly, it came to me
It was a feeling from within
I shared a smile,
I recognized
Love passed by again.
Wykid

BEAUTIFULLY BROKEN

The most beautiful ones have been broken
They've battled through the pain
They've risen from their darkest days
To live and love again.
A heart that has been broken
Grows stronger over time
Mended cracks, leaving scars
Of the pain they left behind.
Don't try to fix the broken
We all heal in different ways
Given time, the wounds will heal
With healing comes brighter days.
In that, we are no different
We all hurt, we all feel pain
We learn from what was broken
When love's light finds us once again.
Wykid

DREAM WALKING

Maybe she will find me
In the middle of her dreams
When sleep has wrapped its arms around her
Creating vivid scenes.
Maybe we can walk together
Along a mountain stream
Maybe she will love me
In the middle of her dreams.
Maybe we can share the night
Go to places we've never been
Maybe she will welcome me
In the middle of her dreams.
Wykid

EMOTIONS IN MOTION

Have you ever felt so broken,
That you found it harder to breathe
Questioning what you thought you knew
Doubting the things you believe?
Have you ever felt like crying?
A tightness gripping your throat
But tears won't fall
Emotions feel empty
Barely keeping afloat.
Watching the world as it's spinning
Happy people at every turn
Finding the lonely, lost in the shadows
Struggling with the lessons to learn.
Driving through the canyon
This thought was weighing on me...
As Autumn kisses the foliage with colors
I miss the forest for the trees.
Wykid

SINK OR SWIM

She feels the waters rising
It's time to sink or swim
Some days the storms are unrelenting
When it comes to her... and him.
She's given all she has to give
Left exhausted in the wake
He's given her nothing in return
All he does is take.
He took her love for granted
He took her happiness in kind
He took away her confidence
He manipulated her mind.
He broke her trust and spirit
He always demanded more
She's barely treading water
Some things she can't ignore.
There is no one there to save her
On herself she must depend
Seeking her own preservation
This madness has to end.
Gasping for her life's breath
She thinks of letting go
Sinking emotionless into the depths
Darkness coming slow.
The thought brings with it teardrops
This can't be the end
Tomorrow the sun will rise for her
Maybe love will find her then.
Wykid

IN THE SHADOWS

He wanted to see her happiness
Though he knew, it wasn't his to share
For him, she walked through his dreams at night
He couldn't help but care
He wanted to see her successes
She didn't know that he stood by her side
Her accomplishments made him proud of her
He stood in the shadows, where he could still hide
He had questions about how things might have been
Had circumstances evolved differently
He held tightly to simple memories
Knowing some things are not meant to be
He can always find a glimmer of hope
When the sun brings about a new dawn
That their eyes might meet
Or she'll share with him a smile
In passing, before she is gone.
Wykid

MISSED CHANCES

I never got the chance to hold her
Hug her, until I carry her scent on me
I never got a chance to kiss her
To taste how sweet her lips must be
I never found the time to tell her
How she travels through my mind
If you could capture what my mind holds
A picture of her is what you'd find
Sometimes I wonder what could have been
Do I invade her dreams at night?
Had I said, or done things differently
Could I have made everything alright?
All I have are my falsified memories
Imaginary days that don't exist
A romance painted without canvas or brush
A love affair dismissed.
Wykid

CHANCE ENCOUNTERS

A look
A glance
A chance encounter
Was all it took to capture my mind
Each day since
Has kept me looking
For something I just can't find
Imagination painting pictures
Vivid, lasting and real
Her taste, so sweet and addictive
Her touch I can almost feel
I lose myself when I think of her eyes
Her journey and stories untold
Her smile captivating me
As her layers begin to unfold
Holding onto memories
That were never lived to be true
I think of them often all the same
They are all that I have left of you.
Wykid

CHANGES

The air is a little crisper
Could it be the winds of change?
Nothing lasts forever
Nothing stays the same
Leaves will soon change color
Cascading to the ground
A cyclical death and dormancy
Creeping in without a sound
I paused
And started thinking
About the world surrounding me...
The changes are inevitable
Some things are meant to be
Aging brings a wisdom
From the loves we've won and lost
Some battles lead to victory
But winning comes with a cost
Somber for a moment
As I stare at the shimmering leaves
Life resembles the Aspen leaf
A falling leaf is me
Growing from roots firmly planted
Branching out on my own
Insignificant, yet important
A single leaf that stands alone
Together we add to the beauty
That makes up the world... and the tree
Alone we fall softly to the ground
Nevermore to be.
Wykid

WINDING ROADS

Forty-seven miles of blacktop
A winding road of memories
Reflections of a past life
A path to a life yet to be seen
Love affairs now distant
Romance that ended before it began
Finding me here, as I watch the sun setting
It's beauty striking me once again
Soon, darkness will overtake me
Night will encompass the sky
Stars will give promise as they shine from the heavens
As today softly whispers goodbye.
Wykid

REBEL SOULS

Nothing is as I remember it
Where are the days I used to know?
Pride has given way to resignation
Gone is the Rebel Soul.
Freedom came with a burning desire
Men fighting for the right and the just
Envisioning a better life
Spilling blood in the mud and the dust.
A flag that stood for something
A reverence for *Our* song as it played
Respect for the President, regardless of side
That's how our country was made.
Once a disciplined nation
Is now chaotic at best
The politically correct and the pandering
Has left behind the rest.
The rest... we are the patriots
We are the 3 percent
We bleed the red, the white, the blue
Love for what they represent.
Education is failing
There is no respect anymore
The justice system is broken
It's simply a revolving door.
I, myself, have grown tired
I'm bitter, angry, and mad
Love of country no longer exists
Leaving me empty and sad.
When push comes to shove, I am fighting
I wonder, which way will you go?
America needs the strong and the proud
She's lost her Rebel Soul.
Wykid

A LOVE THAT FEELS LIKE HOME

With a teardrop falling from her cheek
She puts the last bag in her truck
The end, a new beginning
Perhaps, a change of luck
In a moment of reflection
She replays the last few years
The smiles slowly disappeared
Replaced by nights of tears
As she pulls out of the driveway
She says goodbye one last time
Her past, now in the rearview
Her future, she's yet to find
Anxious, scared, and uncertain
Her mind searching for clarity
Where will she go?
What will she do?
What is meant to be?
Hardships aren't a novelty
They've consumed the life she's known
She wants to find her smile again
She wants a love that feels like home.
Wykid

COLD STEEL

She held her finger on the trigger
She poured another glass of wine
A conversation heard by no one
Helped her pass away the time
Her grievances were many
She'd been wronged like this before
It seemed no matter how hard she tried
They always wanted more
Giving everything she had
Wanting something in return
The more she gave, the more they took
She thought by now she'd learn
A broken heart is fragile
A broken mind beyond repair
Life was lost and hopeless
She had lost the will to care
Some tears fall out of anger
Some fall from the sorrow and pain
She curses, pleads, and barters
As she screams and shouts his name
The fear of starting over
The realization that he is gone
Has left her suicidal
Would anyone miss her when she's gone?
Her finger on the trigger
Cold steel in her hand
She lays the gun on the table
As she tries to understand
Maybe there is someone out there
That will love her for who she is
Someone who will stay when the storms come in
Proud to call her his.
A man who wants to listen
A man that is willing to share
A man who sees her for who she is
A man who truly cares.
Wykid

PIECES OF THE PUZZLE

Putting random words on paper
A mosaic on a page
I wonder,
Are there others like me?
Emotions highly engaged
I'm not sure why I feel them
But I feel them just the same
Love and lust and romance
Sadness, sorrows, and pain
I find it rather conflicting
I'm intense, calculated, and headstrong
Reading the things that I have written
Would indicate that I am possibly wrong
The conflicts that wage inside myself
A perpetual tug of war
Having feelings of indifference
Verses feeling things even more.
I suppose these are the things that make me me
Unique in the life that I lead
A redneck cowboy poet
Painting pictures for others to read.
Wykid

CAPTIVATED

The magic of the moment
A touch that never fades
Memories kept forever—
Things I thought about today.
Radiating smiles
Beautiful eyes in dancing light
A room filled with love and laughter—
Things I thought about tonight.
Words of a conversation
Holding me captive, as they always do
Painting a picture of who you are—
I find myself thinking of you.
Wykid

EMPTY AND HOLLOW

Charlie One Horse pulled down tight
I tip my head into the wind
Miles to go, rivers to cross
Putting distance from where I've been
Snow is blowing sideways
The North wind cuts her path
Bitter windchill biting at my face
I welcome Mother Nature's wrath
I welcome the pain and suffering
I'm not a righteous man
A sinner among sinners
Though living the best that I can
Life has left me jaded
Hardened, calloused, and cold
Like the winter winds that cut through the night
New landscapes will unfold
The path I walk, I walk alone
This is my burden to bear
I remember the warmth of a woman to hold
Yet I find it safer not to care
Busting through the knee-deep snows
No particular path to follow
Black hat collecting the driven snow
Black heart is empty and hollow.
Wykid

MONTANA

One for the Road
Sitting on a barstool
In a rustic old saloon
Coors Light chasing Wild Turkey
It's only half past noon
I put a quarter in the jukebox
E5 for David Allen Coe
I ask the bartender to hit me again
"Give me one more for the road."
Give me one for the woman who left me
Give me one for my broken heart
Give me one for the girl that got away from me
Before my whole world fell apart.
The song had almost finished,
Willie, Waylon and Me,
Taking me back to Montana
And the way things used to be
Picnics by the river
Riding horses in the summer sun
Dressing up on Saturday night
For a little dancing and fun
Falling in love every morning
Making love when the sun went down
Living the life, living the dream
Happy with the love that I found
Shooting back the Wild Turkey
A long draw on the beer
I remember her face; I remember her scent
Even after all these years
Hey bartender, hit me again
Give me one more for the road.
I'm drinking away the memory
To lighten my heavy load

I should have been a better man
I should have seen our lives unfold.
I don't blame her; I'd have left me too
Give me one more for the road.
Wykid

PERFECTLY IMPERFECT

Heavy hearts and fragile minds
Connected late last night
Fortuitous paths of their journeys
Crossing when times were right
The walls are like a fortress
Self-preservation becomes the norm
Hardened, cold, untrusting
Having weathered storm after storm
A man should never shed a tear
He should never show he's weak
I grew up believing this
My conviction's not unique
Yet I have learned in search of self
I'm not the weaker man
There's strength in understanding
In knowing that I can
I cried a tear in pity
Self-loathing and regret
Shedding tears of heartache
For a woman I've never met
Those are the tears that changed me
Unchaining a guarded heart
Still fearful of the future
But not wanting to be apart
Too hard, too fast, too easy
It seems to be my curse
But waiting, wondering, doubting
A pain that felt much worse
A woman should never shed a tear
Questioning where she went wrong
It isn't you; it never was
You were perfect all along.
Perfectly imperfect

I love to hear those words
We all have flaws, things we don't like
But none of mine are hers.
I've said a couple of prayers for you
I got down on one knee
I asked God to provide you happiness
Even if that means it's not with me.
Wykid

BETTER DAYS

The winds of change are cold tonight
Another storm rolls in
It seems that there's no end in sight
When will better days begin?
He looks into his coffee cup
Somber, he just stares
Thinking of what could have been
If she knew how much he cares
Now, time is for reflection
Of the days that made his years
The things that brought him happiness
The things that brought his tears.
She slips away into the night
Carried on the wind,
He prays the storms and currents
Will carry her back to him.
Wykid

YESTERDAYS

Hopscotch on the playground
Playing Four Square, jumping rope
Lost in youthful innocence
Full of dreams and Hope's
Pixie cuts and ponytails
Pretty dresses and bows
She still remembers how cute she felt
As she wonders where time goes
That little girl on the playground
Is now the woman she sees today
She wouldn't mind another chance
To run around and play.
Her life has brought her many things
There's been happiness; there's been tears,
She's proud of the woman she's become
As she reflects on all her years
She feels a tinge of sadness
As she thinks about that girl
The many things she'd like to say
To that little girl in curls.
Wykid

LESSONS

Such ugliness in beauty
Disappointment hides in trust
Betrayal found in friendships
Relationships lost to lust
Innocence deserted
Smiles turn to stone
Eyes you once were lost in
No longer feel like home
Calloused, cold, and jaded
Bridges long since burned
Guarded going forward
With the lessons that were learned.
Wykid

REAL AND RAW

He can't explain the feelings
He only knows he feels
At times, they make it hard to breathe
Emotions raw, so real
It's not a single memory
Or a memory not yet made
That holds him captive to his thoughts
Keeping him enslaved
At times the feelings filter in
He feels them building up inside
Other times they come crashing down
Bringing sorrows he can't hide
To love is something beautiful
Selfless commitment shared in kind
Like chasing rainbows in the dark
Searching for something he can't seem to find.
Wykid

LOST IN TRANSLATION

Words have lost their meaning
When they reach unwanted ears
The touch is cold and lifeless
As days turn into years
Lost in life's translation
The messages transcribed
Expressions masking a loneliness
Behind the listless eyes
Love that once was burning
Now ashes on the ground
Surrounded by isolation
With so many people around
Indiscriminate in its nature
The relationship now no more
Reconciliation becomes stitches
For the way they loved before
Time goes on without them
The sun sets on another day
Opportunities pass them by
In the words they choose not to say
Standing right before them
A new happiness lies in wait
It won't wait forever
Reach out before it's too late.
Wykid

LOVE PASSED BY

It was his time that he was longing to give
With someone who would share theirs in kind
Conversations, real and meaningful
Stimulating hearts and minds
It had been years since he shared his life with a woman
He wasn't searching to find a wife
Though he did seek love and companionship
The old man wanted to share his life
It seemed that time had passed him by
Romance and dating obscure
After a clumsy attempt, he gave up the thought
Rather than proving he's lost and unsure
Confidence once a stronghold
Now wavering, followed by doubt
He watches, he listens, observing
Trying to figure this new dating world out
It felt like a competition—
A game, does everyone play?
What happened to fun conversations,
Learning more as you talk everyday?
Coffee shared in the morning
Maybe ice cream and a short walk
Finding a place to sit together
Sharing more as they continue to talk
Maybe, he thought, he missed his chance
Love of the past is all he will know
Never holding a woman in his arms again
Alone when it's his time to go
It's been a while since I talked to the man
If he found love, I just can't say,
To die alone, the thought saddens me
We are burying him today.
Wykid

COFFEE FOR ONE

Sleep does not come gently
She cries some nights, alone
She tries to place him in her dreams
Where her house becomes a home
Wanting midnight conversations
Talks that are real and from the soul
Learning his dreams, sharing her own
Discovering the life she wants to know
Eventually sleep does find her
Her pillow stained with tears
Sometimes her dreams awaken her
She tries to calm her fears.
Morning all too quickly finds her
An all too familiar scene
Sitting alone, she drinks her coffee
Another day of the same routine.
Wykid

EVERY NOW AND THEN

Every now and then
She gets lost inside her head
Things she used to care about
Now shriveled up and dead
Every now and then
She misses another's touch
She misses the conversations
Sometimes missing them too much
Every now and then
She feels she's lost her reasons why
Nothing feeds the fire inside
It seems that flame has slowly died
Every now and then
She feels lost; she feels confused
Why does happiness avoid her?
Hasn't she paid her dues?
Every now and then
She tries to numb the pain
It doesn't matter in the end
The song remains the same
Every now and then
She tries to fake a smile
It seems to help for a moment
But it fades after a while
Every now and then
She feels like giving up
Half-full or half-empty?
There's nothing in her cup
Every now and then
Her pillow's stained with tears,
She wakes up in the morning
Alone, she'll face her fears.
Wykid

SEARCHING

Looking for the answers
She didn't find them today
Caught up in the confusion
Of a life that went away
She's constantly in search of self
The woman she had become
She misses who she used to be
Before her whole world came undone
Her confidence is shaken
She's lost her identity
Putting one foot in front of the other
Feeling so incomplete
Why was it that he hurt her
Left her isolated and alone?
Why did he choose another woman
Breaking up their home?
Those days are far behind her
She's trying to start life brand new
She'll keep looking for answers
Hoping they lead her straight to you.
Wykid

WINDS OF CHANGE

Changes on the horizon
Changes in the winds
Changes.
Welcoming the thoughts I'm thinking
A chance to start new again
I hold her image close to me
Some things I don't want to change
The way she makes me feel
The way she made me smile
Sometimes,
Life simply needs a rearrangement
I'm not sure where the time went
Though brief,
She left her mark
There's no sadness
There's no anger
Only an emptiness in my heart
If I could,
I'd do things differently
Changing a moment in time
Sometimes less is more
We need mystery
In matters of the heart and the mind.
Wykid

SUNRISE WITH YOU

Lightning strikes without warning
No regard to time or place
A calmness interrupted
Events that cannot be erased
The stillness on the water
Smoke lingering in the air
Words that are heard and spoken
Gentle touches
A moment to care
Sunsets,
Mesmerizing
Nature picture painting the sky
The glow of a fire in the darkness
The silence between you and I
Lost in the time long since passing
Forgotten,
The words and the phrase
Remembered,
The touch and emotions
Reliving,
The nights and the days
The mountains
The stars
And the heavens
Trees,
Skeletal shadows remain
Blessed in the gains and the losses
Smiles mask sorrows and pain
One step at a time slowly taken;
Too fast,
And the race will be done
The stars remain while we are sleeping
Kissed by the morning's new sun.
Wykid

SCARS

Out of the darkness and into the light
Out of sadness, finding a smile
Holding onto the memories
Moving on from the past
Emotions and thoughts reconcile
It's never too early
It's never too late
Grief has a time all its own
It's OK to laugh
It's OK to cry
It's OK to be left all alone
Time will heal all wounds, they say
Wounds that heal leave scars
Scars are reminders of a life that was lived
Lived is the life that is ours
Never forgotten
Never replaced
Never losing their grip on the heart
Always present
Memories never fading
Together
Though in worlds far apart
Embrace the light that's shining
Hear the song the heart wants to play
Live, laugh, and love
The future is waiting
A new life is beginning today.
Wykid

WHISKEY AND WOMEN

He sits the whiskey glass on the table
He finds her number on his phone
He'd really like to talk with her tonight
He's tired,
Tired of being alone.
The miles that separate them
Feel like a million miles away
The lonesome highway beckons him
He's missing her today
He'd leave,
If life would let him
He'd drive all through the night
He could make it to her by morning
Maybe that would make things right
Filling the whiskey glass again
He sets his phone face down
The memories that are haunting him
Are the ones he's trying to drown.
Wykid

NOW AND THEN

I think about her now and then
I wonder how she's been
I wonder if I cross her mind
Does she think of me now and again?
I've still got her number, but I never call
I have notes and letters I never send
Our romance lives inside of my mind
Where things don't have to end.
It's been awhile since I last spoke with her
I'm sure she's moved on by now
As for me, I hold onto the memories
Hoping to relive them somehow.
Wykid

CONVERGENCE

It's beautiful,
Our story,
As I watch it slowly unfold
Remembering hidden feelings
Telling you the things I left untold
It's funny
It's sad
The acts and parts
That make up our own play
It's beautiful,
Our coming together
Our paths leading the same way
I couldn't have written a better story
If I had the words and time
Poetry would fail to capture
The way I feel in rhyme
Sometimes I can't believe it
Some days I simply smile
Something real and something beautiful
That has been missing for a while
I find that I'm thinking of you
Every minute of every day
Enjoying our time together
Missing you when you're away.
Replaying every moment
Every touch that we have shared
Every conversation
Every word that's spoken
Every time you've shown you care
Tonight as we were talking
I stumbled on my words:
"Come here and love me."
I said, "I do."

I wasn't certain that you heard.
Your playful laughter,
Confirmation
You heard the words I said,
I tried to hide
Changing the subject
My thoughts were spinning inside my head.
I'm doing a little better
Trying to suppress the things I say
Tonight,
I answered without thinking
My heart leading me astray.
Wykid

PHOTOGRAPHS AND IMAGES

Sometimes,
A picture or a photograph
Is all we have to hold
Finding comfort in the image
And the emotions they behold
Absent,
Is the physical
Touch merely imagined
The mind creating acts and scenes
Our own fantasies examined
Projecting conversations
Hearing laughter
Finding smiles
Feeling a connection
That's been absent for awhile
A temporary moment
Knowing it's not real
Embracing the envisioned
Holding on to what we feel
Wykid

MAYBE ANOTHER DAY

I can't regret a single thing
When it comes to me and you
I can't forget the memories
The things we say and do
I can't give up the smiles
I can't unhear the sound of your voice
I can't say I love you
Although I do,
I had no choice
I want to walk beside you
But I'm too fast,
I can't slow down
I feel you slipping further behind
Slowly losing ground
Some days find me thinking
That I shouldn't say the things I do
Unsolicited
Unwanted
The things that I tell you
I try to keep a distance
Between my feelings and my heart
But my thoughts and mind won't let me
I miss you when we're apart
Tomorrow might be better
Maybe then you'll say ok
"Show me,
Tell me
That you love me,
You just can't do those things today."
Wykid

A WOMAN'S WARMTH

Evenings come about quicker
The crisp autumn air takes hold
The colors change across the landscape
A new season begins to unfold
The warmth of a fire radiating
Shadows dancing on amber walls
Dim lighting creates an ambience
A romance comes with fall
Four Roses, neat, in a whiskey glass
A romantic vision uncovered
Drifting thoughts go back in time
When nights were shared with another
There's something unmistakable
About a woman's love and tender ways
Her warmth and kindness
Her calming presence
Her comfort at the end of the day
The past, just a bygone season
Those days have long ago expired
I welcome the changes, come as they may
As I put another log on the fire.
Wykid

ACTS AND SCENES

No words spoken
A subtle touch
A moment passing in time
A silent look
An unforced smile
Playing out in my mind.
Act to act
Scene to scene
The curtain failing to close
Drawn to the romance
Intrigued by the story
The finale remaining unknown
Caught in the clutch of the dreamer
No intermission when it comes to the heart
Alone,
I watch from the mezzanine
Waiting for the next play to start.
Wykid

TIME ALONE

Today,
We took a walk together
I held her hand in mine
We walked along a mountain stream
She shared with me her mind
We shared our laughter
We shared our smiles
We shared stories
We reminisced
We shared our dreams
We shared past heartaches
With me,
She shared a kiss.
Today,
We took a Sunday drive
Exploring sights unseen
Driving slow
With nowhere to go
Discovering places that we've never been.
Today,
I spent my time alone
Silent conversations
And thoughts filled with smiles
Romancing the dreams
Getting lost in the visions
That I found in each passing mile.
Wykid

CLOUD 9

Words paint beautiful pictures
I lose myself in the stories I tell
Love and romance
Passions and dreams
Reliving memories I remember so well
Every happy ending once had tragedy
A love lost or a heart that was broken
The happiness reflected in poem
Hiding the pain of words left unspoken
I understand that I'm anything but typical
I don't really know where my story begins
The way that I think
The things that I feel
The man that I keep caged within
Life, in all of her beauty
Is a fickle bitch, it seems,
Riding cloud 9
Unaware
Unexpecting
Of the pain and the heartbreak she brings.
Still,
I find I care deeply
Finding reasons to live, love, and smile
Enjoying the people
Enjoying the ride
Happiness finding me once in a while.
Wykid

TIME AND PLACE

Precious moments
Precious memories
Precious time slowly erased
Visions fade
Dreams start to vanish
Leaving not a trace
What I had and what I wanted
Were not matched in time and place
I'll never travel far enough
To forget her pretty face
I can see her in the distance
I can see her behind closed eyes
I'm with her when the sun is setting
Sharing coffee with each sunrise
No matter where my journey takes me
I carry her along
Every poem and every lyric
Every stanza
Every song.
Wykid

TIMELESS

Timeless...
Thoughts and images
Pictures in my mind
Endless...
Dreams and fantasies
Picturesque
Flirting with sublime.
Wykid

PIECES OF YOU

I want to hold a piece of you
A little something of my own
To walk among your thoughts and dreams
When you're feeling all alone
It won't be something tangible
It won't be something real
Let me infiltrate your deepest thoughts
When your body aches to feel
Let me walk with you in summer rains
Mental rapture when you call
Planting seeds of passion in the spring
Reaping the rewards of you each fall
When winter's chill is biting
And darkness comes too soon
Welcome me with open arms
Behind the locked door to your room
When life has left you wondering
When nothing is going right
Close your eyes and I'll be there
To hold you through the night.
Wykid

MUSIC AND MELODIES

The emotions that are now in motion
Playing a song my heart can hear
A rhythmic, lyrical story
A masterful balladeer
I listen to each note intently
Getting lost in their harmonic wave
Each word telling the tale of my life
Lost and broken
Now found and saved
There are no instruments playing
No voices singing the songs that are heard
Yet I hear them,
I sing along to them
I can understand every word
The smile that I share is revealing
I love the new love I have found
The music keeps time with my heart beating
A beautiful melody not making a sound.
Wykid

MILE MARKER 126

Miles of highway for contemplating
Wandering thoughts fill idle time
Reflecting on my observations
She has a beautiful mind
Running my fingers over her past
Discovering things once unknown
Lingering on the parts that intrigue me
Embracing the parts she has shown
Her story,
In words,
Fill the pages
The pages,
Hold the story to tell
Her novel,
Only partially written
Each chapter
Keeping me compelled
My questions,
Although, some go unanswered
An invitation
To share what she will
What she shares
Has purpose and meaning
Beautifully honest and real.
Wykid

TATTERED AND TORN

Alone, with just the thoughts in my head
A peculiar place to be
The merry-go-round keeps spinning
Moving further away from me
Here in this silent suffrage
Where truth and fiction collide
A hope and a prayer
Grasping for anything
That makes me feel something inside
I long ago gave up on the dreaming
The figures kept fading away
Caught in my mind for a moment in time
Always knowing that they wouldn't stay
Miles pass by on the blacktop
Thoughts crashing like a mid-summer storm
A dark cloud passing over me
Taking with it,
A love, tattered and torn
Occasionally, testing the waters
Sometimes blindly, just jumping in
Real and raw in the honesty
Knowing that I'll sink or swim
Seldom and few are the real conversations
Saved for a meaningful exchange
It seems there is no one there to listen
My words,
Are they foreign and strange?
Barely treading water
No life preserver in sight
I take a deep breath,
Holding it in,
Driving down the highway tonight.
Wykid

HOW DO YOU WANT TO BE LOVED?

How do you want to be loved?
Can you answer without delay?
Do you know what you want?
Do you know what you need?
Do you find it easy to convey?
Do your scars illicit a smile?
Memories of a life lived through the years
Adventures in love
Heartache and loss
Happiness and sorrow found in your tears
Do you embrace yourself as a woman
Confident in who you've become?
Satisfied,
Knowing you've done your best each day
As you watch the setting sun
How do you want to be loved,
Can you share your secrets with me?
Take my hand in yours
Let's walk for a while
Tell me what it is that you see.
Wykid